My role in society,
or any artist's or
poet's role, is to try
and express what we
all feel. Not to tell
people how to feel.
Not as a preacher,
not as a leader,
but as a reflection
of us all.

john lennon's
little book of
selected quotes

It's fear of the unknown.
The unknown is what it is.
And to be frightened of it
is what sends everybody
scurrying around chasing
dreams, illusions, wars,
peace, love, hate, all that-
it's all illusion. Unknown is
what it is. Accept that it's
unknown and it's plain
sailing. Everything is
unknown-then you're ahead
of the game. That's what it is.
Right?

john lennon's
little book of
selected quotes

Strawberry Fields
is anywhere you
want to go.

john lennon's
little book of
selected quotes

Tame birds sing
of freedom.
Wild birds fly.

john lennon's
little book of
selected quotes

There was something
wrong with me,
I thought, because I
seemed to see things
other people didn't
see.

john lennon's
little book of
selected quotes

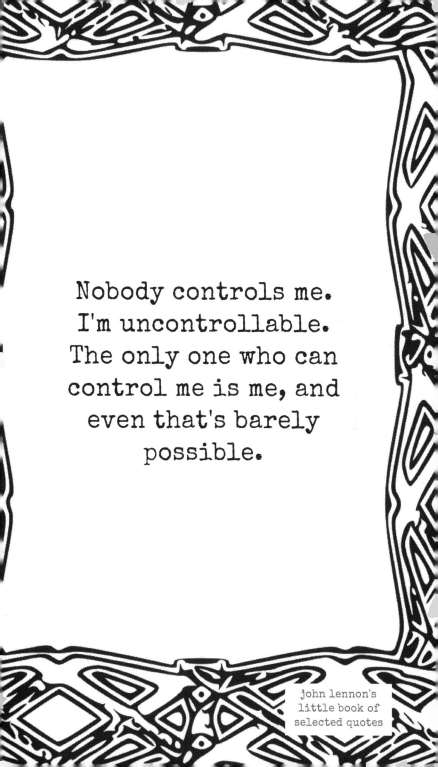

Nobody controls me.
I'm uncontrollable.
The only one who can
control me is me, and
even that's barely
possible.

john lennon's
little book of
selected quotes

Life is what happens
while you are busy
making other plans.

john lennon's
little book of
selected quotes

Produce your own dream. If you want to save Peru, go save Peru. It's quite possible to do anything, but not if you put it on the leaders and the parking meters. Don't expect Carter or Reagan or John Lennon or Yoko Ono or Bob Dylan or Jesus Christ to come and do it for you. You have to do it yourself.

We need to learn to love ourselves first, in all our glory and our imperfections. If we cannot love ourselves, we cannot fully open to our ability to love others or our potential to create.

john lennon's little book of selected quotes

As I play the game of life, I try to make it better each and every day. And when I struggle in the night, The magic of the music seems to light the way.

john lennon's little book of selected quotes

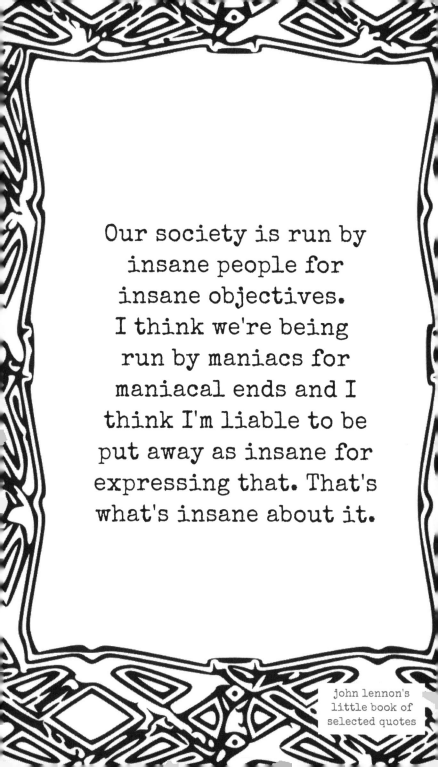

Our society is run by insane people for insane objectives.
I think we're being run by maniacs for maniacal ends and I think I'm liable to be put away as insane for expressing that. That's what's insane about it.

john lennon's little book of selected quotes

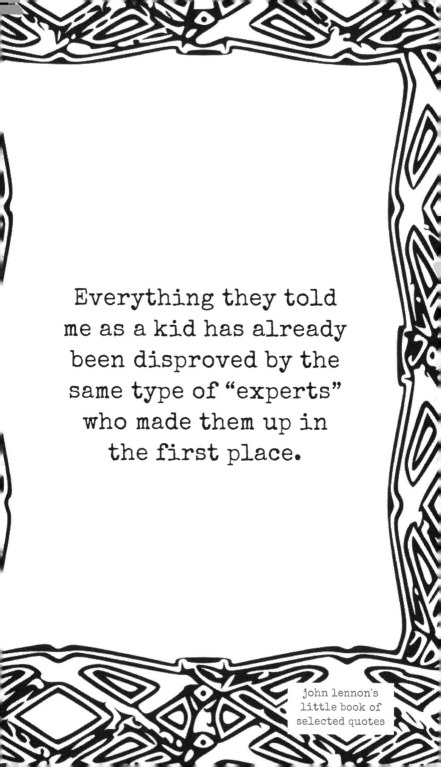

Everything they told me as a kid has already been disproved by the same type of "experts" who made them up in the first place.

john lennon's little book of selected quotes

Possession isn't nine-tenths of the law. It's nine-tenths of the problem.

john lennon's little book of selected quotes

paranoia is just a
heightened sense
of awareness

john lennon's
little book of
selected quotes

Love is a promise,
love is a souvenir,
once given never
forgotten, never
let it disappear.

john lennon's
little book of
selected quotes

Love is the answer,
and you know
that for sure;
Love is a flower,
you've got to
let it grow.

john lennon's
little book of
selected quotes

Yeah we all shine on,
like the moon, and the
stars, and the sun.

If the masses started to accept UFOs, it would profoundly affect their attitude towards life, politics, everything. It would threaten the status quo. Whenever people come to realize that there are larger considerations than their own petty lives, they are ripe to make radical changes on a personal level, which would eventually lead to a political revolution in society as a whole.

john lennon's little book of selected quotes

I believe in everything until it's disproved. So I believe in fairies, the myths, dragons. It all exists, even if it's in your mind. Who's to say that dreams and nightmares aren't as real as the here and now?

john lennon's little book of selected quotes

We've got this gift of love, but love is like a precious plant. You can't just accept it and leave it in the cupboard or just think it's going to get on by itself. You've got to keep watering it. You've got to really look after it and nurture it.

john lennon's little book of selected quotes

I would like to say thank you on behalf of the group and ourselves and I hope we've passed the audition.